D0053877

A Note to Parents

DK READERS is a compelling program for beginning readers, designed in conjunction with leading literacy experts, including Dr. Linda Gambrell, Professor of Education at Clemson University. Dr. Gambrell has served as President of the National Reading Conference and the College Reading Association, and has recently been elected to serve as President of the International Reading Association.

Beautiful illustrations and superb full-color photographs combine with engaging, easy-to-read stories and informational texts to offer a fresh approach to each subject in the series. Each DK READER is guaranteed to capture a child's interest while developing his or her reading skills, general knowledge, and love of reading.

The five levels of DK READERS are aimed at different reading abilities, enabling you to choose the books that are exactly right for your child:

Pre-level 1: Learning to read

Level 1: Beginning to read

Level 2: Beginning to read alone

Level 3: Reading alone

Level 4: Proficient readers

The "normal" age at which a child begins to read can be anywhere from three to eight years old. Adult participation through the lower levels is very helpful for providing encouragement, discussing storylines, and sounding out unfamiliar words.

No matter which level you select, you can be sure that you are helping your child learn to read, then read to learn!

LONDON, NEW YORK,
MELBOURNE, MUNICH, AND DELHI

For Dorling Kindersley
Project Editor Heather Scott
Designer Hanna Ländin
Brand Manager Lisa Lanzarini
Publishing Manager Simon Beecroft
Category Publisher Alex Allan
Production Controller Nick Seston
Production Editor Sean Daly

For Lucasfilm
Executive Editor Jonathan W. Rinzler
Art Director Troy Alders
Keeper of the Holocron Leland Chee
Director of Publishing Carol Roeder

Reading Consultant
Linda B. Gambrell, Ph.D.

This book is dedicated to Edie Beecroft

First published in the United States in 2008
by DK Publishing
375 Hudson Street
New York, New York 10014

09 10 11 10 9
SD346—05/08

DK Books are available at special discounts when purchased in bulk
for sales promotions, premiums, fund-raising, or educational use.
For details, contact: DK Publishing Special Markets,
375 Hudson Street, New York, New York 10014
SpecialSales@dk.com

Published in Great Britain by Dorling Kindersley Limited.
A catalog record for this book is available from the Library of Congress.

ISBN: 978-0-7566-4083-5 (Paperback)
ISBN: 978-0-7566-4084-2 (Hardback)

Color reproduction by Alta Image, UK
Printed and bound in the U.S.A. by Lake Book Manufacturing, Inc.

Discover more at
www.dk.com
www.starwars.com

DK READERS

STAR WARS

THE CLONE WARS™

Watch out for Jabba the Hutt!

Written by Simon Beecroft

This is Anakin Skywalker.
He is a brave Jedi.

Anakin travels all over
the *Star Wars* galaxy.

He meets many different
people and creatures.

Would you like to
meet them, too?

Before we start, Anakin wants to tell you something important.

He says that you must be careful. Anakin is always on his guard.

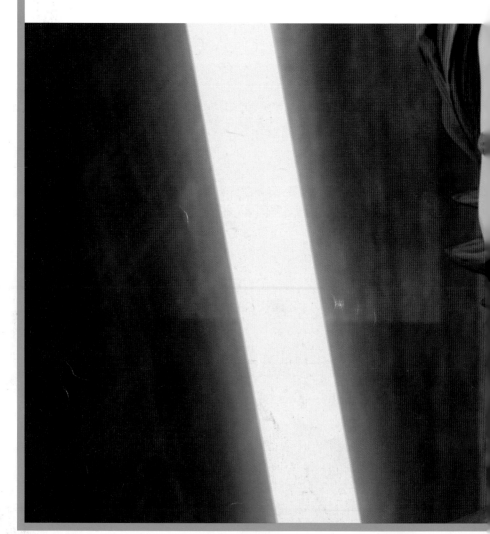

Most people and creatures are friendly, but some are not.

Jabba the Hutt is not friendly, so if you see him—watch out!

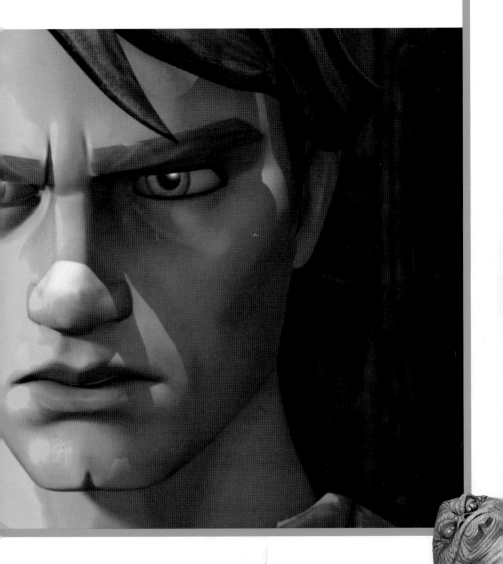

First let's meet Anakin's
friend, Ahsoka.

Ahsoka is brave and clever.

Anakin and Ahsoka travel
everywhere together.

They look after each other.

Ahsoka is learning to be a Jedi,
and Anakin is her teacher.

Now let's say
hello to R2-D2.

R2-D2 is a
clever machine.

He can fly
spaceships and
fix things.

Anakin and R2-D2 fly
together in a spaceship.

R2-D2 can even blast himself into
the air!

Here are some more of
Anakin's friends.

Obi-Wan is a Jedi Master.
He taught Anakin how to
be a Jedi.

Yoda is one of the most powerful Jedi. He is small but very strong and wise.

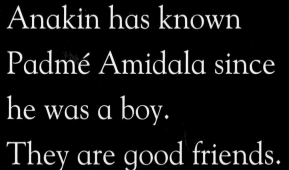

Anakin has known Padmé Amidala since he was a boy. They are good friends.

Captain Rex is a soldier.

Rex wears a helmet on his head.
He wears armor on his body.

Rex leads a big group of soldiers.

Anakin and Rex go
into dangerous
battles together.

Watch out!
These machines are not friendly.

They are robots called
battle droids.

Luckily, they are
not very dangerous.

In battle they often get confused.
Then they fall over
or run the wrong way.

These creatures are very dangerous.

General Grievous is in charge of a big army of battle droids.

He has angry yellow eyes.

Ventress fights with lightsabers.

She wants to fight Anakin.

She sends her green
spy droid to spy
on Anakin.

Quick, let's
run away.

Oh no! Now we've run into a rancor!

A rancor is a big monster with sharp teeth and claws.

It stands up on its hind legs and might try to eat you!

Anakin will protect you with
his lightsaber.

If you thought the rancor was dangerous, what about this swamp monster?

The swamp monster lives underwater.

But it can also jump out of the water onto land.

Look out—it wants to get you!

These Jedi will protect you!

Jedi Master Plo Koon wears a face-mask.

He fights with a blue lightsaber blade. He has long fingers.

Luminara Unduli has green skin.

She fights with a green lightsaber blade.

Be careful. This is Ziro the Hutt.

His body is covered in glowing patterns.

Ziro is
in charge
of a gang
of criminals.

He likes to capture people
and lock them up.

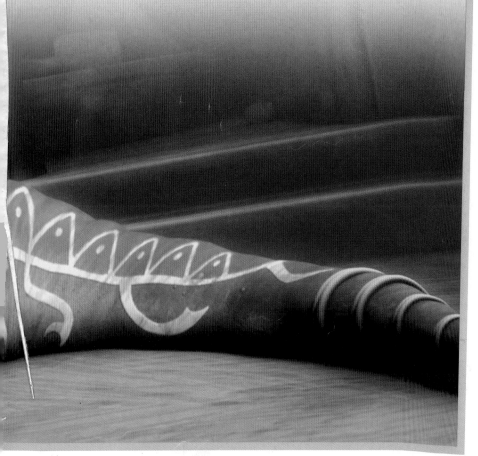

Now we're in trouble.
It's Jabba the Hutt.

Jabba is Ziro's nephew.

They pretend to be friends,
but really they are enemies.

Everyone is scared of Jabba.
Even Jabba's droid servant is
scared of him.

You can never
trust a Hutt!

Jabba is cruel
and mean,
but he loves
his son, Rotta.

Perhaps Jabba is not all bad.

Anakin is not so sure.

He says you
should always
WATCH OUT FOR
JABBA THE HUTT!

Who are they?

Anakin
He's a
good Jedi.

Ventress
She's angry and
dangerous.

Jabba the Hutt
He is big, bad, and
cruel, but his son,
Rotta, loves him!

Ahsoka
She's learning to
be a good Jedi.